AF632131

Tavi Khan – The Blue Tiger

OrangeBooks Publication

1st Floor, Rajhans Arcade, Mall Road, Kohka, Bhilai, Chhattisgarh 490020

Website:**www.orangebooks.in**

© Copyright, 2026, Author

All rights reserved. No part of this book may be reproduced, stored in a retrieval system, or transmitted, in any form by any means, electronic, mechanical, magnetic, optical, chemical, manual, photocopying, recording or otherwise, without the prior written consent of its writer.

First Edition, 2026

ISBN: 978-93-7426-734-9

Price: Rs. 549.00

The opinions/ contents expressed in this book are solely of the authors and do not represent the opinions/ standings/ thoughts of OrangeBooks or the Editors .

Printed in India

TAVI KHAN

THE BLUE TIGER

THE JOURNEY BACK HOME

Aryan Prathap

OrangeBooks Publication
www.orangebooks.in

Dedicated to

My sister Aradana & little brother Athiyan

Tavi Khan – The Blue Tiger

The journey back home

Chapter 1: The Whispering Wind

In the middle of a big green forest, there was an old temple. Vines and moss covered it. The walls had strange shapes and old pictures. The wind liked to blow through the cracks and make soft sounds.

Inside the temple, under the moonlight, slept a very special tiger.

His fur was bright blue. His eyes were shiny silver. His name was Tavi Khan. He didn't know where he came from.

Tavi had lived in the temple since he was a baby. One rainy morning, he had woken up at the temple gate. He was alone. He was wrapped in leaves, and a small bell hung from his neck on a red string.

He didn't know who put it there. He didn't know anything about his past.

The forest took care of him. The wind told him stories. The temple watched him like a friend.

But today felt different.

That morning, the wind whispered something new.

"Tavi... come home..." It was quiet, but Tavi heard it. He felt a shiver. "Home?" he whispered. "Isn't this my home?"

He stood up. The bell on his neck made a soft sound. Sunlight came through the trees. The forest was waking up.

Tavi took a deep breath. It was time to find out where he really came from.

Tavi walked through the forest. The birds were singing. Leaves moved in the breeze. Monkeys were making lots of noise.

Then—SPLAT!

A mango flew through the air and hit a tree.

Tavi blinked and licked the juice from his whiskers. "Mmm, tasty," he said. Another mango flew by.

"Hey!" Tavi shouted. "Stop throwing fruit!"

A tiny voice called out, "Go away, blue fur!"

Tavi looked up. A monkey was sitting on a branch, wearing yellow goggles. His name was Ziggy.

"You're in the land of Ziggy the Mango Bandit!" he said. "Drop your bananas or get mango-smacked!"

“I don’t have bananas,” Tavi said. “What’s on your face?”

Ziggy jumped down. He fell flat but stood up like nothing happened.

“These? Goggles. Night vision. Mango-vision. I made them.”

Tavi looked closer. “They’re made from coconuts and bottle caps.”

"Exactly. Very rare," Ziggy whispered.

Tavi tried not to laugh.

"So who are you?" Ziggy asked. "You look like a tiger who fell in blue paint."

"I'm Tavi Khan," the tiger said. "I'm looking for my real home."

Ziggy's ears twitched. "Ooo, a real home? Sounds fun. I'll help you!

" He tapped his goggles. "Let's go, Bluebell."

"It's Tavi."

"Sure, sure. Let's go, Tabby."

And just like that, the Blue Tiger and the Mango Bandit became a team— one brave, one silly, both ready for an adventure they didn't expect.

They had walked into a part of the forest that even Ziggy had never seen.

“This place is weird,” Ziggy whispered.

Tavi sniffed. “It smells like moss... mushrooms... and... mint?”

Suddenly, the trees opened up. In the middle of the clearing was a giant tree with funny leaves shaped like question marks.

A sign on the tree said: THE RIDDLE TREE.

Speak true, answer right, or sneeze for a night.

Ziggy read it. “Sneeze for a night? That’s strange.”

Then a loud voice said,

“WHO IS AT THE RIDDLE TREE?”

The ground shook a little. Tavi stepped forward. "I'm Tavi Khan. And this is Ziggy—"

"THE MANGO BANDIT!" Ziggy said proudly. The tree moved. A small hole opened like an eye.

"To pass," the voice said, "you must answer a riddle!"

Ziggy gasped. "Yes! I love riddles! Kind of." The riddle was:

"What has a face and two hands, but no arms or legs?"

Ziggy shouted, "Spaghet—wait. No, not spaghetti."

Tavi walked in circles. "A face... two hands... no arms or legs…" Suddenly, his bell jingled. He stopped.

"It's a clock!"

The tree was quiet.

Then it shouted, "CORRECT!"

It sneezed and shot out a little confetti.

"BLEHH-CHOO! Sorry," said the tree. "I'm allergic to myself." A path of shiny stones lit up.

Ziggy cheered. "We did it! We beat a talking tree!"

"You almost said spaghetti," said Tavi.

"That would've been silly," Ziggy smiled.

They followed the glowing path, hoping to find Tavi's real home.

****

Chapter 2: The Mango Bandit

Tavi and Ziggy walked along the glowing path from the Riddle Tree. The forest around them looked different now. The trees were taller. The air felt warmer.

"Do you even know where we're going?" Ziggy asked, poking a leaf with his tail.

"No," said Tavi. "But I think the wind does." Ziggy blinked. "The wind? You're following air?"

Tavi smiled. "It whispered to me. It said, 'Come home.'"

Ziggy scratched his head. "Wow. My belly just whispers 'snack time.'"

As they walked, the glowing stones started to fade. Soon, they were just regular stones.

"Uh-oh," Ziggy said. "No more glowing rocks. We're on our own now." Suddenly, Tavi's paw hit something soft and squishy.

SQUELCH!

He looked down. "What is this?"

Ziggy bent down and picked up a big, muddy piece of old cloth. "Looks like a blanket."

"No," said Tavi. He shook the cloth, and the mud dropped off. "It's a map!"

The map had weird shapes, dotted lines, and a picture of a mountain with a giant eye.

At the bottom, it said:

TO FIND WHAT'S LOST, FOLLOW THE MOSS.

Ziggy tilted his head. "Who writes poems on a map?"

"Someone who wants us to find something," Tavi said.

Ziggy looked around. "Moss, moss... where's the moss?"

Tavi pointed. "There. It's growing on the trees. All on one side." "So we follow the moss!" Ziggy shouted, pumping his fists. "Shhh!" Tavi whispered. "You'll wake the forest."

Too late

From behind a bush, something growled.

Tavi and Ziggy froze.

Out stepped a small, grumpy-looking badger with a leaf on its head like a hat.

"Who steps on my nap spot?" the badger grumbled.

"Uh… sorry," Ziggy said. "We didn't see you!"

The badger sniffed. "You're noisy. And muddy. And you smell like mango."

Ziggy smiled. "Thanks! That's my natural smell."

Tavi stepped forward. "We're looking for a mountain with an eye. Do you know where it is?"

The badger scratched its chin. “Maybe I do. Maybe I don’t. Maybe I’m sleepy.”

Tavi tilted his head. “Please?”

The badger yawned. “Fine. I’ll tell you. But first... bring me something sweet.”

“Like candy?” Ziggy asked.

"No," said the badger. "Like honey. Fresh honey."

Ziggy gasped. "Honey? That means... BEES!" The badger smiled. "Buzz buzz."

Tavi looked at Ziggy. "Still want to be my guide?"

Ziggy sighed. "Let's find that honey."

And off they went again—one step closer to the mountain, one bee sting away from the next clue, and one tiny badger who might (or might not) know the way home.

****

Chapter 3: The Honey Hunt

Tavi and Ziggy walked through the forest, looking for honey. The badger had told them that he would help if they brought him something sweet. And what could be sweeter than fresh honey?

The buzzing sound grew louder, and they saw a large tree with a big, golden hive hanging from one of the branches. The bees were busy flying around, carrying the golden nectar.

"We need that honey," Tavi said, his eyes fixed on the hive.

"I see it!" Ziggy whispered, his voice filled with excitement. "But… how do we get it without the bees getting angry?"

"I'm not sure," Tavi replied, "but we'll have to be careful."

Ziggy scanned the ground and found a big, flat leaf. Tavi picked up a long stick. Together, they tiptoed toward the tree.

The bees flew all around them, not noticing the two adventurers sneaking closer. Ziggy and Tavi held their breath, hoping the bees wouldn't spot them. They managed to reach the tree and used the stick to nudge the hive gently. But just as Tavi reached for the honeycomb, a bee landed right on Ziggy's nose!

Ziggy froze.

"Don't move," Tavi whispered, his heart racing.

The bee buzzed around for a moment before it flew away, leaving Ziggy unharmed. He let out a sigh of relief.

"Phew, that was close," Ziggy whispered. "Let's get that honey."

Finally, Tavi scooped up some honey into the big leaf, making sure not to spill any. It was sticky and golden, and the sweet smell filled the air.

But just as they were about to leave, the bees noticed them.

Buzz! Buzz! Buzz!

The bees swarmed toward them, angry at the thieves.

"Run!" Ziggy shouted, his voice high-pitched with panic.

Tavi grabbed the honey-filled leaf and dashed through the forest. Ziggy scampered behind, his small legs moving fast. The bees followed, buzzing angrily, but

Ziggy and Tavi were too quick. They jumped over rocks, dodged trees, and ran through the thick forest.

Suddenly, the ground beneath them gave way, and with a loud splash, they both fell into a muddy pond. The bees stopped chasing them. They didn't like water.

Tavi and Ziggy looked at each other, covered in mud and laughing.

“We did it,” Tavi said, grinning. “We still have the honey!”

But just as they were about to stand up, a soft voice interrupted them. “What are you two doing in my pond?” it asked.

A turtle’s head popped up from the water, blinking slowly at them.

“We’re sorry,” said Tavi. “We didn’t mean to fall in. We’re on a journey to find my home.”

The turtle looked at them curiously, then nodded slowly. “A journey, huh? Sounds interesting. But you’re all muddy now, aren’t you?”

Ziggy grinned. “Muddy is my natural look!”

Tavi smiled and held out the leaf with honey. “We brought this honey for the badger. He said he would help us if we gave him something sweet.”

The turtle blinked again. “Honey, you say? That’s a good trade. My name’s Tama. You can call me Tama the

Turtle. I'm very smart, you know. Maybe I can help you with your journey."

Tavi's ears perked up. "Really? You'd help us?"

Tama nodded. "Yes, yes. Follow me. I know this forest like the back of my shell."

The three new friends set off together—Tavi, the blue tiger; Ziggy, the funny monkey; and Tama, the wise turtle. They followed the path back to the badger, who was waiting for them near the edge of the forest.

The badger smiled and grabbed the honey. "I'll help you now. Follow the river up ahead to the mountain. That's where you'll find the answers you seek."

Tavi looked at the map again. The mountain on the map had a big eye carved into it. It seemed like the place where everything would finally make sense.

****

Chapter 4: The Mountain with One Eye

Tavi, Ziggy, and Tama walked for what felt like forever. The path was steep, and the air grew cooler as they climbed. The forest around them started to change, with tall trees giving way to rocky cliffs. They followed the river as the badger had instructed, and soon, they reached a place where the land seemed to rise up in front of them.

At first, it seemed like just another mountain. But as they drew closer, the shape of the mountain became clearer. It had a large, round cave at the top that looked like a giant eye staring down at them.

The mountain was silent, and the wind was cold, but something about it felt special.

"This must be it," said Tavi, his voice soft with awe. "This is the mountain with one eye."

They began their climb. Ziggy scampered up the rocks with ease, while Tama climbed carefully on Tavi's back, slowly and steadily.

Tavi focused on the path ahead, his heart pounding with excitement. The climb was hard, but they kept going. With each step, Tavi felt like he was getting closer to the answers he had been searching for all this time.

At the top, they found something glowing. A large stone, shaped like a bell, sat in the middle of the cave. As soon as Tavi approached it, his bell, the one he had worn since he was a baby, began to shine too bright and warm.

Then, the stone did something unexpected. It began to glow even brighter, and pictures appeared in the air, swirling around them. Tavi blinked in surprise.

He saw two tigers, one with strong muscles and proud eyes, the other with soft, kind eyes. They were looking at a tiny blue tiger cub. The cub was him.

Tavi's heart raced as he watched the images. "They're my parents," he whispered.

The pictures changed again. He saw the temple, the red string, the bell— everything he remembered from his childhood.

The pictures showed how his parents had hidden him in the temple to keep him safe, because there was danger. And after he was hidden, they had been searching for him ever since.

Tavi's eyes filled with tears, but they weren't tears of sadness. They were tears of hope and joy. He had found the answers he had been looking for. His parents hadn't forgotten him. They had been searching for him all along.

The images faded slowly, leaving only the soft glow of the stone. Tavi turned to his friends. "I know where to go now," he said, his voice filled with confidence.

The wind blew gently, like a soft hug. Tavi felt it, and he knew that home was closer than ever before.

With their hearts full, they began the long journey down the mountain, the path now lit by glowing fireflies that danced in the air, guiding their way. Tavi looked up at the sky, and for the first time, he truly believed he was on his way home.

****

Chapter 5: The Bell, the Breeze, and Home

Tavi, Ziggy, and Tama followed the glowing fireflies as they fluttered through the trees.

The forest seemed different now. The air was softer, and the sky was beginning to change colours as the sun started to set. The wind whispered in Tavi's ears, as if it were excited too.

It felt like they were being guided, as if the wind was gently urging them forward.

The journey had been long, but now, it felt like they were close to something very special. Tavi's heart beat faster with each step. His bell jingled softly around his neck, and he felt a warmth spread through him. He had a feeling that home was just around the corner.

They passed through tall grass that swayed in the breeze, crossed a calm stream that sparkled in the fading light, and walked beneath trees with silver leaves that shimmered like stars.

It was a peaceful path, one that made Tavi feel calm, but also excited. He was getting closer.

And then, they saw it.

A beautiful green valley stretched out before them. Flowers of all colours bloomed in the fields, and waterfalls tumbled down rocks in the distance, creating a soft, soothing sound. In the middle of the valley was a small hill, and standing at the top of the hill were two tigers.

Tavi stopped in his tracks. His eyes widened.

There, standing under the golden light of the setting sun, were his parents. One tiger was tall and strong, with a proud look in his eyes. The other was smaller, but her eyes were kind and full of love. They looked just like the pictures he had seen on the mountain, and Tavi knew, deep down, that they were his family.

The moment his parents saw him, their eyes filled with tears. They started running toward him, their paws swift on the soft grass.

Tavi's heart fluttered. He didn't move at first. He just stood there, staring at them, feeling all the love he had been missing for so long. His bell rang softly in the wind, a sound like a welcoming tune.

His parents reached him, and without saying a word, they wrapped their paws around him. Tavi squeezed his eyes shut, feeling their warmth, their love. He was home.

"You came back," his mother said, her voice gentle and full of emotion.

"We never stopped looking for you," his father added, his voice strong but tender.

Tavi's eyes filled with tears, but this time they were happy tears. He felt safe, loved, and finally, he was where he belonged.

Ziggy and Tama stood back, watching the reunion with smiles on their faces. Ziggy clapped his hands excitedly, and Tama gave a slow, wise nod.

Tavi turned to them, his heart full. "This is my family," he said, his voice soft with pride.

His parents smiled warmly at his friends. "And your friends are welcome here too," his mother said, her voice as kind as the breeze.

That night, they all sat together on the soft grass, under a sky full of twinkling stars. They had a big dinner, with mangoes, honey cakes, and sweet berries. The air was filled with laughter and music.

Ziggy and Tama told funny stories, and even Tavi joined in, laughing and playing with his new family. It felt like a celebration of everything they had all been through to get here.

As they sat around the fire, Tavi looked up at the stars. He could hear the sound of the waterfall in the distance and the rustling of the leaves in the trees. Everything felt peaceful, just like the stories the wind had told him.

For the first time in his life, Tavi felt a sense of completeness. He had found his parents, made new friends, and discovered his true home. He knew that this was the beginning of a new chapter in his life, one full of love, adventure, and happiness.

He smiled to himself as he closed his eyes, the gentle breeze caressing his fur.

He was home.

And he would live happily ever after.

***** THE END *****